Animal Disguises

KINGFISHER

LONDON & NEW YORK

Copyright © Kingfisher 2010
Published in the United States by Kingfisher,
175 Fifth Ave., New York, NY 10010
Kingfisher is an imprint of Macmillan Children's Books, London.
All rights reserved.

Distributed in the U.S. by Macmillan, 175 Fifth Ave., New York, NY 10010
Distributed in Canada by H.B. Fenn and Company Ltd.,
34 Nixon Road, Bolton, Ontario L7E 1W2

First published as *Kingfisher Young Knowledge: Animal Disguises* in 2004
Additional material produced for Kingfisher by Discovery Books Ltd.

Library of Congress Cataloging-in-Publication data has been applied for.

ISBN 978-0-7534-6451-9

Kingfisher books are available for special promotions and premiums.
For details contact: Special Markets Department, Macmillan,
175 Fifth Avenue, New York, NY 10010.

For more information, please visit www.kingfisherbooks.com

Printed in China
10 9 8 7 6 5 4 3 2 1
1TR/0410/WKT/UNTD/140MA/C

Note to readers: the website addresses listed in this book are correct at
the time of going to print. However, due to the ever-changing nature
of the Internet, website addresses and content can change. Websites
can contain links that are unsuitable for children. The publisher cannot
be held responsible for changes in website addresses or content or
for information obtained through a third party. We strongly advise
that Internet searches be supervised by an adult.

Acknowledgments

The publishers would like to thank the following for permission to reproduce their material. Every care has been taken
to trace copyright holders. However, if there have been unintentional omissions or failure to trace copyright holders,
we apologize and will, if informed, endeavor to make corrections in any future edition.
b = bottom, *c* = center, *l* = left, *t* = top, *r* = right

Cover main Shutterstock/Kristina Postnikova; cover *l* Shutterstock/Sergey Khachatryan; cover *r* Shutterstock/Olga Utlyakova; page 1 Ardea;
3 Naturepl; 4–5 Naturepl; 7 Naturepl; 8*b* Getty Images (Getty); 9*t* Oxford Scientific Films (OSF); 10–11 Ardea; 11*t* Ardea; 11*b* Corbis; 12 Nature
History Picture Agency (NHPA); 13*tr* Getty; 13*cl* OSF; 13*b* Corbis; 14*cl* OSF; 14*b* OSF; 15*tr* Fogden Photographs; 15*b* Naturepl; 16*tr* Ardea; 16*b* OSF;
17 Fogden Photographs; 18–19 Naturepl; 18*tl* Naturepl; 19*tr* Fogden Photographs; 20–21 Corbis; 20*b* Ardea; 21*br* Ardea; 22–23 National Geographic
Image Collection; 22*cl* NHPA; 23*tr* OSF; 24–25 National Geographic Image Collection; 24*bl* Ardea; 24*br* Ardea; 26*b* OSF; 27*t* Naturepl; 27*b* Naturepl;
28*cr* Fogden Photographs; 28*bl* OSF; 29*tr* OSF; 29*b* Corbis; 30*tl* Ardea; 30*b* Ardea; 31*t* Ardea; 31*br* Ardea; 32–33 Getty; 32*bl* Fainting Goat Association,
U.S.A.; 33*tr* National Geographic Image Collection; 34*t* Ardea; 34*b* Corbis; 35 Ardea; 36–37 Ardea; 36*bl* OSF; 37*tr* Naturepl; 38–39 Ardea; 38*bl* Ardea;
39*tl* NHPA; 39*tr* NHPA; 39*b* Ardea; 40 Corbis; 41 Naturepl; 41*t* Corbis; 48*c* Shutterstock Images/Eric Isselee; 48*b* Shutterstock Images/Ostill;
49*t* Shutterstock Images/Lori Froeb; 49*b* Shutterstock Images/Ecoprint; 52*t* Shutterstock Images/Grant Terry; 52*l* Shutterstock Images/Sam
Chadwick; 53*l* Shutterstock Images/John Swanepoel; 53*b* Shutterstock Images/Iarus; 56 Shutterstock Images/Kristian Sekulic

Commissioned photography on pages 42–47 by Andy Crawford
Thank you to models Anastasia Mitchell, Holly Hadaway, and Sonnie Nash

Animal Disguises

Belinda Weber

KINGFISHER
NEW YORK

Contents

What is camouflage?

Camouflage is the way an animal blends in with its surroundings. It can be the animal's body shape or the color of its coat or skin that helps it match its home. Camouflage is used for two reasons—to hunt and to hide from predators.

Silent power

Creeping through the undergrowth, a tiger is difficult to see. The long grass is light in color, but its shadows look black. The light and dark lines blend in with the markings on the tiger's back.

Spots and stripes

Spots and stripes break up an animal's shape. At dusk or dawn, when many creatures feed, their markings blend in with the shadows, making it difficult to see each animal clearly.

Who's who?

A zebra's coat confuses predators. All the stripes merge, and it is hard to see where one zebra ends and another one begins.

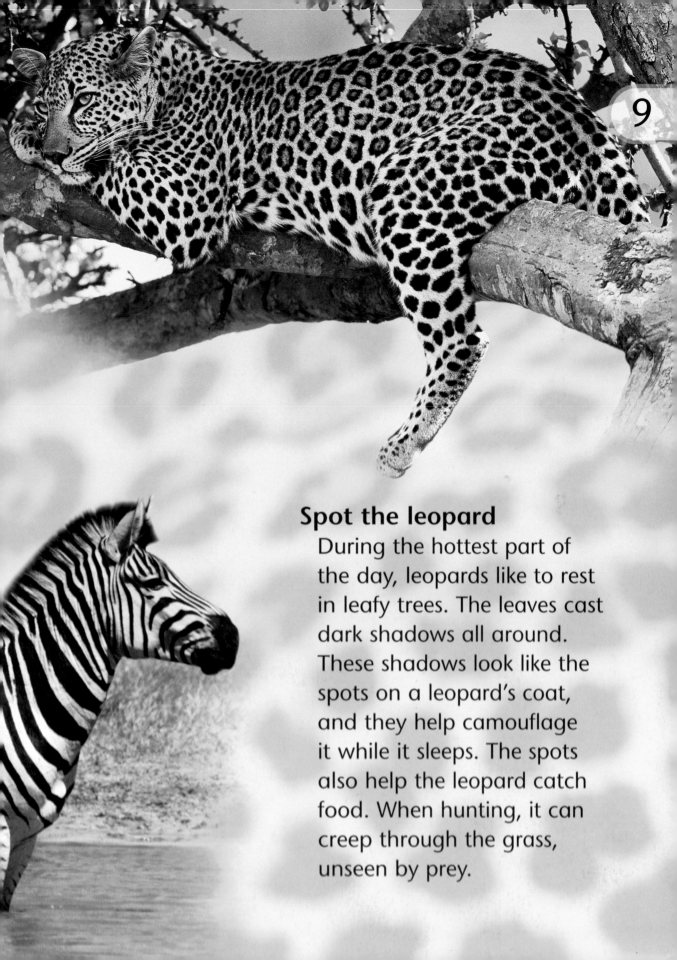

Spot the leopard

During the hottest part of the day, leopards like to rest in leafy trees. The leaves cast dark shadows all around. These shadows look like the spots on a leopard's coat, and they help camouflage it while it sleeps. The spots also help the leopard catch food. When hunting, it can creep through the grass, unseen by prey.

Blending in

Bold colors and shapes are great disguises. In wooded areas, where there is a lot of light and shade, strong markings make it difficult to see what is a shadow and what is an animal.

Standing tall
The dark blotches on a giraffe's coat look like patches of shade. They help disguise it as it feeds on the acacia trees in its African habitat.

Safe in the grass

When it is first born, a baby red deer cannot run fast enough to keep up with its mother. The mother deer hides it in grasses where its spotted brown coat matches the light and shadows on the ground.

Super stripes

Tapirs live in rainforests. For the first six months of their lives, baby tapirs have striped coats that make them difficult to see in the dappled jungle light.

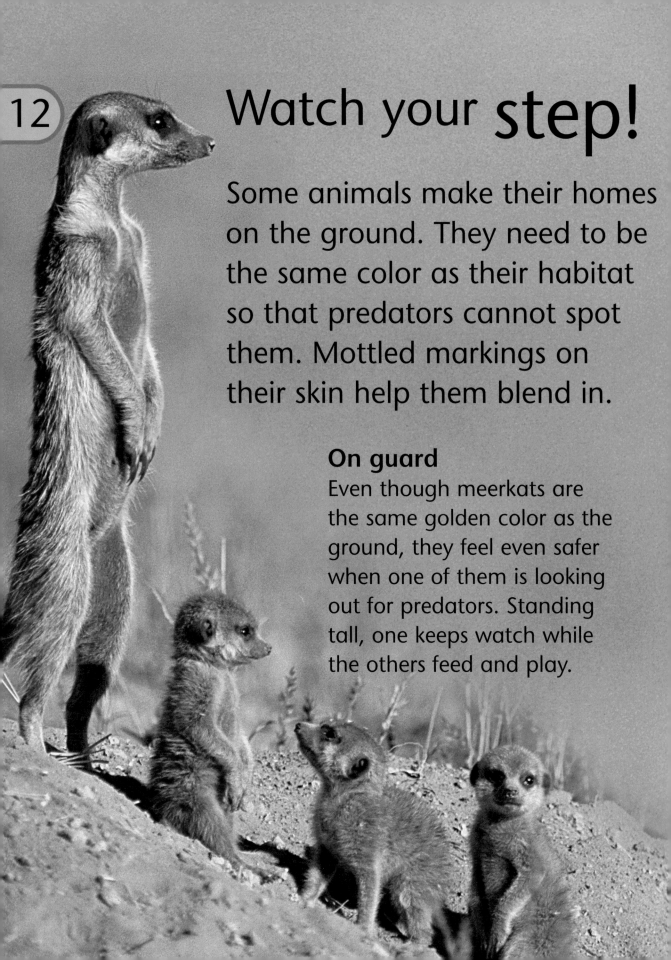

Watch your step!

Some animals make their homes on the ground. They need to be the same color as their habitat so that predators cannot spot them. Mottled markings on their skin help them blend in.

On guard

Even though meerkats are the same golden color as the ground, they feel even safer when one of them is looking out for predators. Standing tall, one keeps watch while the others feed and play.

Living carpets

Carpet sharks look like the seabed. This is because the blotchy patches on their skin match the rocks and stones around them.

In hiding

Pheasants' feathers are multicolored, so it is difficult to see them in the shade. They hide in wooded areas or in long grass.

Froggy floors

Marsupial frogs live among the fallen leaves in rainforests. Their brown patchy skin makes them difficult to see. Even the babies look like the forest floor.

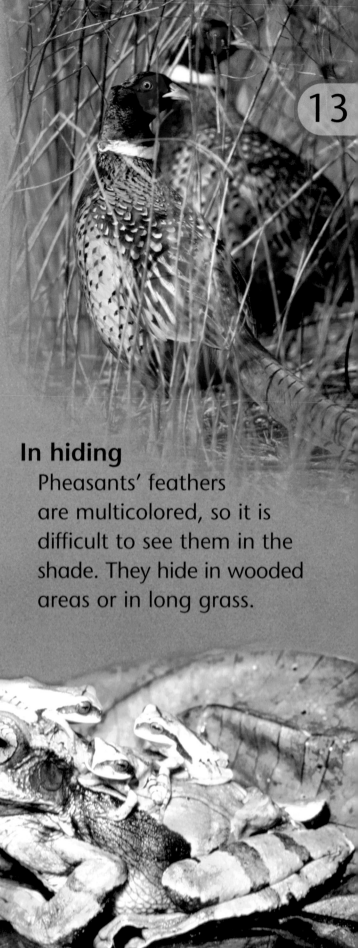

Life in a leaf

Leaves make good hiding places. Some animals hide there to catch prey by surprise. Others eat the leaves and do not want to be seen by predators.

Leafy looks

The body, legs, and head of this wandering leaf insect are shaped just like the leaves it eats.

Dead ringer

The leaf-tailed gecko scampers across the forest floor. Its body shape and color make it look like dead leaves.

Life on the riverbed

The Suriname toad blends in perfectly with the leaves that blanket the riverbed where it lives. It hides, camouflaged, waiting for passing prey.

Lacy lichen

Lichen katydids live in tropical cloud forests. They merge almost seamlessly with the lichen plants that grow there. The feathery leaves of the plants match the lacy pattern on the katydid's body.

Flowers and fruit

Plants often have bright flowers and tasty fruit. They need animals to help them spread their seeds. But even the prettiest flower is not always what it seems.

Pretty in pink

Lurking in this bright pink flower, a crab spider waits for a tasty meal. It holds its front legs wide apart, ready to grab its prey.

Watch out!

Hidden among the white flowers, this orchid mantis is difficult to see. If an insect flies by, the mantis will attack and eat the welcome snack.

Fruit surprise

This tasty-looking palm
fruit hides a deadly secret.
Waiting silently among the
fruit, an eyelash
viper hopes
its prey will
come within
easy striking
distance.

Stony features

A large number of creatures live among rocks and pebbles. The different colors of the stones and the shadows they cast make great hiding places.

Stone home

An African rock python is difficult to see among the stones. Its skin is mottled, so it matches the colors of the rocks perfectly. It rests on the stones while it warms itself in the sun and then slides off quietly in search of prey.

Jumping stones

Stone grasshoppers have such good disguises that they are often visible only when they move. Their long back legs allow them to make powerful jumps, so they can leap away from predators.

Star spotting

The stargazer fish buries itself in the seabed to complete its disguise. The only things that give it away are its eyes and mouth, but even these look like pebbles and sand. Fish that swim too close are snapped up for a tasty meal.

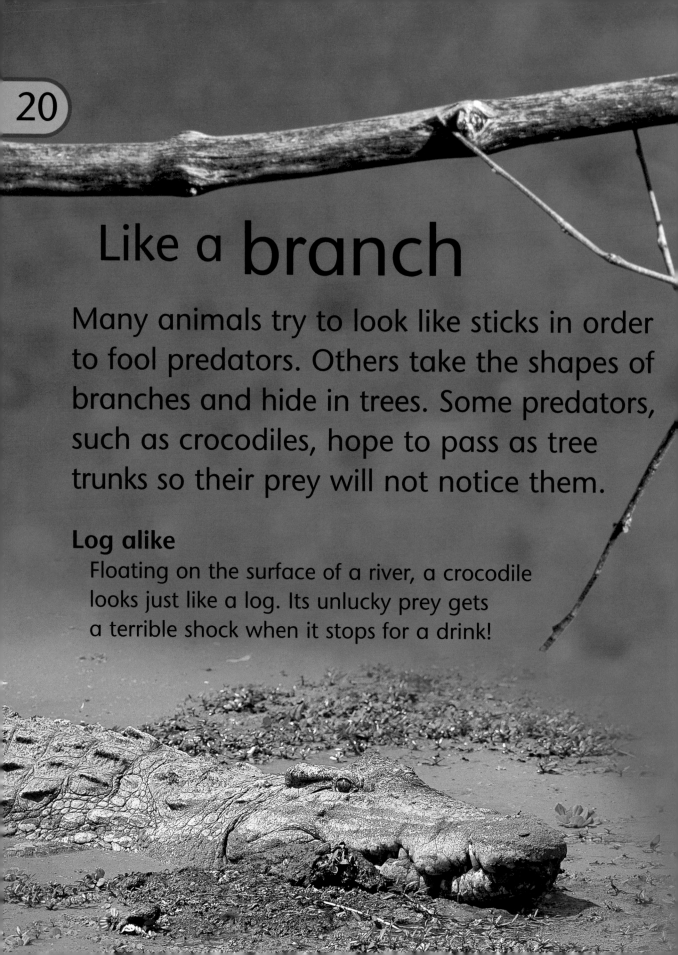

Like a branch

Many animals try to look like sticks in order to fool predators. Others take the shapes of branches and hide in trees. Some predators, such as crocodiles, hope to pass as tree trunks so their prey will not notice them.

Log alike

Floating on the surface of a river, a crocodile looks just like a log. Its unlucky prey gets a terrible shock when it stops for a drink!

Walking stick

With its long, thin body
and legs, a stick insect
is easily confused with
a twig. It even sways
gently in the wind—
just like a twig does!

Slowly, slowly

Clinging upside down to
branches, a sloth creeps
around its forest home.
When it rains, algae grow
on the branches and in
the sloth's fur, helping
it hide in the trees.

Above and **below**

Some animals have light-colored stomachs and dark backs. This is a double disguise called countershading. It makes them difficult to see both from above and from below.

Light and dark

The lapwing has a dark gray-green back that blends in with grass. This makes it tricky to see from the air. But when it flies, the lapwing's white belly blends in with the light sky, so it is difficult to see from the ground.

Black and white

When it swims,
a penguin's white
belly blends in with
the lighter surface water.
From above, its dark back
looks like deep water.

Sneaky sharks

Sharks and other fish use countershading,
too. A shark is able to sneak up on a school
of fish from above or below because its dark
and light coloring helps disguise its shape.

New season's colors

Camouflage works only if the animal looks like its surroundings. When the weather changes, some animals have to change their coat color so that they still look the same as their habitat.

The latest look

Snowshoe hares live in Alaska. In the summer, their coats are brown to blend in with the ground. In the winter, the hares grow new white coats to help them stay hidden in the snow.

A new winter coat

Arctic foxes are predators and need to be able to sneak up on their prey. In the winter, their snowy white coats blend in perfectly with their icy world. In the summer, their coats are brown, so they match the earthy colors of the season.

Time to change

Chameleons are the masters of disguise. Special cells in their skin let them change their skin color to match their background. Some chameleons can switch colors in fewer than 20 seconds.

parson's chameleon

antsingy leaf chameleon

Colorful creatures

Chameleons are predators and need to stay hidden until they attack their insect prey. Whether resting in leaves or hunting in the desert, a chameleon can change its skin color to match its background.

desert chameleon

Shape shifters

Sometimes, skin color and shape are not enough to keep an animal hidden. Sticks, stones, plants, and even clothes may be used to make a new disguise.

Living garden

Darkling beetles cover their bodies with lichen and other small plants. These grow and help the beetles stay hidden from predators as they search for food.

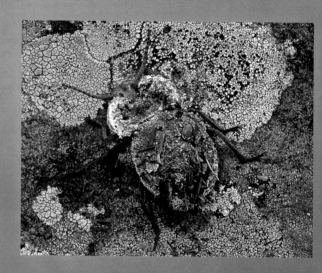

Skilled weaver

The clothes moth larva does not like to be disturbed while it is feeding. It makes itself a coat out of whichever sweater it is eating and then feasts without interruption!

Making a shell suit

A caddis fly larva's disguise is a case that grows around its body. On top of this clever camouflage, the larva sticks shells, small pebbles, leaves, or any other small items it can find.

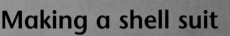

Hanging decorations

A decorator crab's body is covered with tiny hooked hairs. It hangs seaweed from these hairs to help it hide on the seabed.

Eye disguises

An animal's eyes are very sensitive. If they are attacked, it can cause blindness and put the creature's life in danger. For this reason, some animals have "false eyes." Others hide their eyes with bold patterns.

Eyes down

Fruit bats like this one (above) rest in large groups and often squabble. To protect their eyes during fights, they have white tufts of hair beneath their ears. Attackers target these instead of the real eyes.

Heads or tails?

The eyes of butterfly fish are hidden in a dark stripe across their faces. They also have a false eye near the tail, so predators attack the wrong end.

How many eyes?

The eyespots on this emperor moth's wings look like eyes. If a predator attacks them, it is unlikely to do much harm, and the moth can escape.

Looking back

This pearl-spotted owlet has false eyes made from dark feathers on the back of its head. These decoy eyes may confuse both predators and prey about which way the owl is looking.

Playing tricks

Some animals have an extra defense when attacked. They behave strangely or do something unexpected that confuses the predator and stops it from attacking.

All fall down

Fainting goats perform a nifty trick when they feel threatened—they fall over in a dead faint! Once the danger has passed, the goat gets up as if nothing happened.

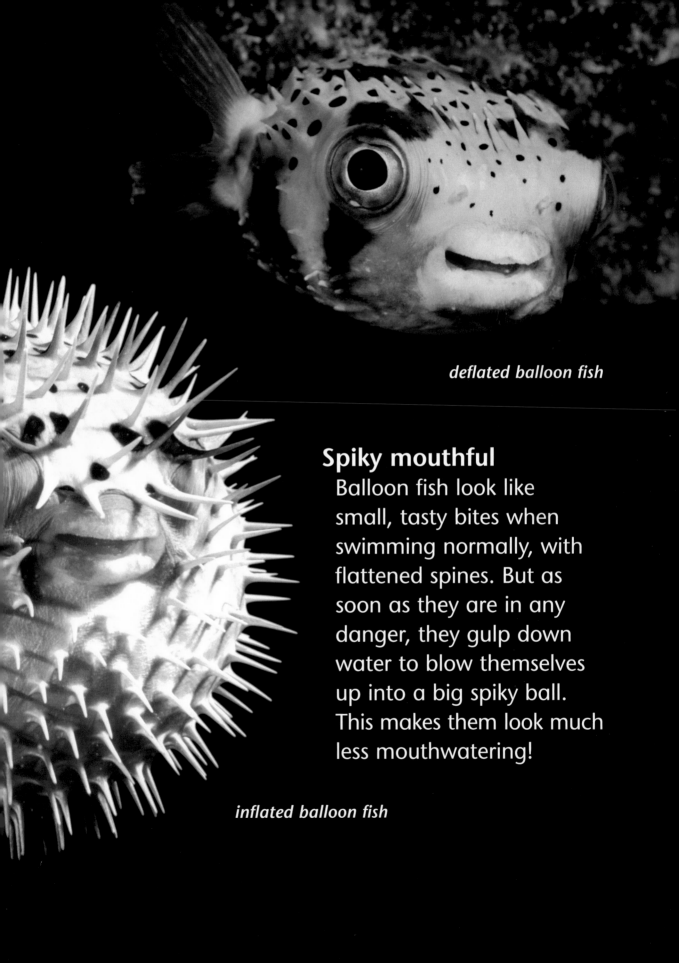

deflated balloon fish

Spiky mouthful

Balloon fish look like
small, tasty bites when
swimming normally, with
flattened spines. But as
soon as they are in any
danger, they gulp down
water to blow themselves
up into a big spiky ball.
This makes them look much
less mouthwatering!

inflated balloon fish

Surprise!

Sometimes, a predator holds off eating an animal if it is startled in some way. Many animals rely on surprising their attacker, and then they escape.

Which way around?

The shingleback lizard's tail looks like its head! Attackers that mistakenly go for the tail may find that the lizard escapes in the other direction.

Flashing red

At rest, a fire-bellied toad looks like floating pondweed. But when it is startled, it rears up and flashes its red and black belly.

Frills

A frilled lizard has a flap
of skin around its neck
that opens like an
umbrella when
it is scared.

Terrible traps

Some predators are so well disguised that prey comes too close, unaware of any risk. Others bring their prey within striking distance using a trap, or lure.

Wagging tongues

The pink tip of this alligator snapping turtle's tongue wriggles like a worm. If a fish swims up to eat the worm, that fish becomes the turtle's dinner!

Tempting tails

The yellow end of a copperhead snake's tail looks like lunch to a frog. But if it gets too close, the frog itself ends up on the menu.

End of the line

Anglerfish live in deep, dark oceans. They lure prey with a "fishing line" that hangs over their mouths. The end of the line glows. Fish come to look at the light and are eaten by the sneaky anglers.

Clever copies

Predators learn what tastes bad or is poisonous and then avoid it. Some prey animals mimic, or copy, bad-tasting objects or animals. Predators then steer clear of them, too.

No sting in the tail!
Bees, wasps, and hornets have painful stingers, so predators avoid them. This clearwing moth looks like a hornet, and this keeps it safe from predators.

Copy ant
Ants produce a poison to stop attackers. The mirid bug looks like an ant, and this protects it.

Pueblan milk snake

eastern coral snake

Mix up

Coral snakes are highly venomous. Milk snakes are harmless, but they look like the coral snakes. This means that most attackers leave them both alone.

Not what it seems

Some predators are clever mimics. This praying mantis looks like a bird dropping! If an insect comes close, it soon gets snapped up.

Hide-and-seek babies

Baby animals are often left alone while the parents search for food. To keep them safe, their colorings blend in with their surroundings.

Sitting pretty

Lion cubs have sandy-colored coats that match their savanna home. They hide in the grass while their mother is away.

Hard to spot

Arctic tern chicks wait for their parents to bring them food. Their feathers look like the surrounding rocks, allowing them to blend in. The small chick beside the chirping one shows just how good this camouflage is.

Snow babies

Harp seal cubs live in icy places. Their white coats help them hide on the snowy ground until they are big enough to defend themselves.

Hidden homes

Make a caddis fly larva's house

Caddis fly larvae live underwater. They make a camouflaged case in which to live. The case is made out of whatever they can find in the pond or stream where they live. They carry the case around with them and hope that no one will notice them. You can make a disguised home for a model caddis fly larva.

You will need:
- Cardboard tube
- Brown paint
- Paintbrush
- Glue
- Camouflage material: twigs, leaves, shells, stones
- Modeling clay—3 colors
- 1 yellow pipe cleaner

1

Mix some brown paint and water. Take the cardboard tube and paint it brown. Leave it to dry. This is your caddis fly larva's case.

2

Glue small twigs, dried leaves, shells, and small stones onto the cardboard tube. Make sure the tube is well covered. Leave it to dry.

3

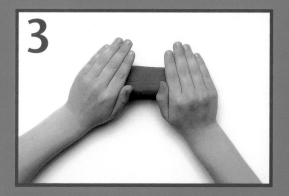

Roll some blue modeling clay into a sausage shape. Make sure it is small enough to fit inside the tube. This is the larva's body.

4

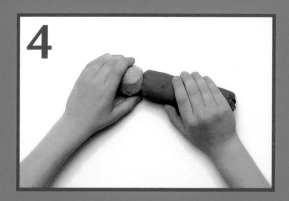

Take a smaller piece of light blue modeling clay and roll it into a ball. Attach it to the darker blue body. Your larva now has a head!

5

Using some green modeling clay, make two tiny flat balls for the eyes and a small cone for the mouth.

6

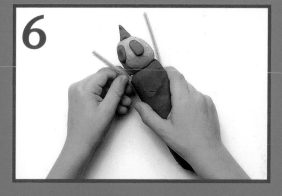

Cut a pipe cleaner in half and push one piece into each side of the body. The larva is now ready to be put inside its new home.

Tiger fun

Tiger face painting

Paint your own face while looking in a mirror. Or draw tiger stripes on a friend's face and then ask him or her to paint your face.

You will need:
- Face paints and paintbrushes
- Warm water
- Soap
- Sponge

Start with a clean face! Put black face paint on a brush. Paint the tip of your nose and your lips. Draw a stripe beneath your nose.

With white paint, draw whiskers coming out from under your nose, across your cheeks, and around the corners of your mouth.

Paint black stripes under your eyes and on your forehead, chin, and cheeks. Add white stripes on your eyebrows and a dot on your nose.

4

Use red and orange paints to fill in some lines on your cheeks, chin, and forehead.

Add the finishing touches with some gold paint on your forehead, cheeks, and chin. Now that you look like a tiger, it is time to test the disguise. How many people recognize you with a tiger's face?

When you have had enough of being a tiger, carefully wash off the face paints using warm water, soap, and a sponge.

Mystery picture

Draw a camouflage picture

Chameleons are masters of disguise, and these two are no exception. In this clever two-in-one picture, you will need two outlines of a chameleon. To get the basic shape, you could trace around the parson's chameleon on pages 26–27.

1

Color in one of the chameleon pictures in shades of green and blue. Use purples and oranges for the second chameleon picture.

You will need:
- 2 pieces of 8 ½ x 11 inch paper, each with an outline of a chameleon on it
- Colored markers
- Ruler
- Pencil
- Scissors
- A piece of paper that measures at least 11 x 17 inches
- Glue

2

Add backgrounds to both pictures. Then, using a ruler and a pencil, draw lines down both pictures that are about one inch (3 centimeters) apart.

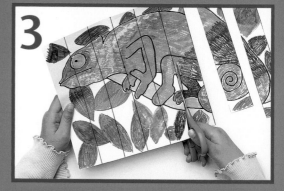

3

Carefully cut along the lines so that your pictures are in long, thin strips. Stack them in order, with the chameleon head on top.

4 Take the long piece of paper. Glue the top strip of the green picture on the left. Next to it, paste the first strip of the purple picture. Continue doing this until there are no strips left. When the paper is dry, fold the new picture along the edges of the strips, into a zigzag shape.

Look at the picture from the right, and you will see the green chameleon.

Look at it from the left, and there is the purple chameleon.

Glossary

alga—a tiny, plantlike organism (plural: algae)

blend—to match the surroundings

cell—tiny unit from which all living things are made

cloud forest—a tropical mountain rainforest

coat—the skin and fur of an animal

dappled—patterned with spots or patches of a darker color

decoy—something that is designed to mislead

earthy—brown

faint—to collapse or pass out

glow—to shine brightly

habitat—the area where an animal or plant lives

inflated—blown up, like a balloon

larva—the young stage of some animals' life cycles

lichen—a plantlike organism made of a fungus and algae

lure—an attractive-looking trap

mimic—to copy

mottled—having a pattern of colored blotches or stripes

predator—an animal that hunts and eats other animals

prey—an animal that is hunted and killed by another animal

savanna—stretches of dry grassland in tropical areas

school—a large group of fish swimming together

seabed—the bottom of the sea or ocean, usually covered with sand, rocks, and stones

sensitive—easily damaged

startled—surprised

tropical—an area near the equator where it is hot all year long

venomous—poisonous

visible—easy to see

This book includes material that will be useful to teach and reinforce certain elements of science and language arts curricula in the elementary grades. The topic provides many opportunities for crosscurricular connections with art.

Extension activities

Language arts
Art/writing/oral language
Design an imaginary animal that is well suited to a habitat of your choice. Draw your animal so that it blends in with its surroundings. Write an explanation of your animal's particular camouflage adaptations and present a short report to your class.

Writing
Choose a creature from this book and write a one-page story about a hunt in which its camouflage plays a part. Write from the perspective of the predator. Then retell the story, this time writing from the perspective of the prey.

Art
1) Numerous examples of countershading (pp. 22–23) can be found in open ocean dwellers such as sharks, tuna, dolphins, and whales. Make a watercolor wash for a background and create a chart of some of these fish and mammals, showing their special coloration.

2) Use the illustration of the emperor moth on p. 31 as a model for size and shape. Cut out several such moths from white paper. Color in each one so that it blends in closely with some spot in the room. It must be in plain view but as hard to see as possible because of its protective coloration. Challenge your classmates or family members to find your moths.

Science
The topic of animal disguises relates to the scientific themes of diversity, adaptation, structure and function, interdependence, and interaction with the environment. Some specific links to science curriculum content

include behavior (pp. 6–9, 10–21, 26–39, 42–43); predator/prey relationships and survival (pp. 6–7, 14–21, 30–31, 34–35, 38–39); environments and ecosystems (pp. 8–9, 10–13, 24–25, 42–43); and life cycles (pp. 11, 40–43).

Using the projects
Children can do these projects at home. Here are some ideas for extending them:

Pages 42–43: Caddis fly larvae live in aquatic environments such as streams and ponds. What type of water environment do you think best suits your model?

Pages 44–45: What other animal faces could you paint? If you would like to keep your animal face, make a mask by cutting eye and nose holes in a large paper bag and paint directly on the bag.

Pages 46–47: Chameleons are not the only animals that can change color. Some others with this nifty ability include the four-spotted flounder, the mimic octopus, the golden tortoise beetle, and the seahorse. Research to find out more about these animals and create camouflage pictures for them, too.

Did you know?

- One type of caterpillar from Costa Rica frightens would-be attackers by mimicking a dangerous snake.

- Not all camouflage is visual. Some animals roll around in the dung of other animals to disguise their own scent.

- The arctic fox is the only member of the dog family that changes the color of its fur.

- Orchid mantises are born with black and orange bodies. Their color changes as they grow older, depending on the colors of their surroundings.

- There are more than 3,000 different species of stick insects around the world.

- The eggs of the stick insect are some of the largest in the insect kingdom—some reach more than 0.3 inches (8 millimeters) long.

- Some hunters use scent to fool their prey. The bolas spider produces a scent similar to that of a female moth, which attracts male moths into its trap.

- The stomach of the hatchet fish glows with a light blue color, the same color as sunlight when it shines down into the ocean. This makes the hatchet fish almost invisible to predators below it.

- A zebra's stripes make it easy to see when it's standing still, but when it's moving, the stripes make a blur that confuses predators.

- Balloon fish are not only dangerous because of their spikes and inflated bodies, they are also among the most poisonous animals in the world. One fish contains enough poison to kill 30 people.

- The young of many mammals, including lions and pigs, have camouflage markings. They disappear as the animals get older.

- Male chameleons often "fight" one another by competing to show off their brightest colors.

- Every single zebra has a unique stripe pattern. Zebras identify one another this way.

- Even some plants use camouflage: the "living stone" plants found in African deserts look almost exactly like pebbles.

Animal disguises quiz

The answers to these questions can all be found by looking back through the book. See how many you get right. You can check your answers on page 56.

1) Where do tapirs live?
   A—deserts
   B—rainforests
   C—grassland

2) What color is a zebra?
   A—black and white
   B—black and yellow
   C—red and blue

3) Where do leopards like to rest on very hot days?
   A—in the river
   B—in long grass
   C—in leafy trees

4) Where do crab spiders sometimes catch their prey?
   A—on the seashore
   B—in tall trees
   C—in flowers

5) How does the stargazer fish camouflage itself?
   A—it buries itself in the seabed
   B—it hides behind bigger fish
   C—it looks like seaweed

6) How do chameleons change color?
   A—they have special cells in their skin
   B—they shed their skin and grow a new one
   C—they rub themselves with green leaves

7) What color is the arctic fox in the winter?
   A—brown
   B—white
   C—green

8) Where are the false eyes on a pearl-spotted owl?
   A—on its tail
   B —on its stomach
   C—on the back of its head

9) What is the body of the balloon fish covered in?
   A—spots
   B—spikes
   C—stripes

10) Which animal uses a "fishing line" to catch its prey?
    A—anglerfish
    B—fruit bat
    C—praying mantis

11) What does the clearwing moth disguise itself as?
    A—an ant
    B—a crab
    C—a hornet

12) What do darkling beetles cover themselves in?
    A—shells
    B—lichen
    C—leaves

Find out more

Books to read

Animal Hide and Seek (DK Readers) by
    Penny Smith, Dorling Kindersley, 2006
*Clever Camouflage (Animal Attack and
    Defense)* by Kimberley Jane Pryor,
    Macmillan Education, 2009
Everything You Need to Know about Animals
    by Nicola Davies, Kingfisher, 2010
First Fun: Animal Encyclopaedia by Steve
    Parker, Philip Steele, Jane Walker, and
    Brian Ward, Miles Kelly Publishing,
    2004
The 10 Best Animal Camouflages by
    Cameron Lindsey, Children's Press, 2008

Places to visit

San Diego Zoo, San Diego, California
www.sandiegozoo.org
Come face to face with a wide range of
animals, check out the Polar Bear Plunge
and Discovery Outpost, and even enjoy
a zoo sleepover.

Indian River Reptile Zoo, Canada
www.reptilezoo.com/zoo/index.html
Discover more about reptile camouflage
at Canada's amazing reptile facility. You
can see the country's largest rattlesnake
collection, as well as the Serpentarium
and Alligator Alley.

Smithsonian National Zoological Park,
Washington, D.C.
http://nationalzoo.si.edu
Visit 2,000 animals from 400 different
species and learn more about animal
habitats and camouflage, from the

brightly colored poision-arrow frogs of
the Amazon to great cats the color of
savanna grasses.

Websites

*http://ngm.nationalgeographic.com/2009/
08/mimicry/ziegler-photography*
View "The Art of Deception," an
incredible collection of animal kingdom
photographs on the *National Geographic*
website, featuring toads that look like
leaves and caterpillars with "false"
heads.

www.bronxzoo.com
Learn more about animals in their
natural habitats, painstakingly recreated
at the Bronx Zoo. View slideshows, listen
to podcasts, and watch videos of
animals at the zoo.

http://animal.discovery.com
Check out the website of TV's Animal
Planet to find the best zoos in the United
States and learn to identify butterflies,
mammals, and wild birds.

Animal disguises
quiz answers

1) B   7) B
2) A   8) C
3) C   9) B
4) C   10) A
5) A   11) C
6) A   12) B